Discrimination *in Society*

Age Discrimination

Carla Mooney

ReferencePoint
Press®

San Diego, CA

About the Author

Carla Mooney is the author of many books for young adults and children. She lives in Pittsburgh, Pennsylvania, with her husband and three children.

For more information, contact:
ReferencePoint Press, Inc.
PO Box 27779
San Diego, CA 92198
www.ReferencePointPress.com

LIBRARY OF CONGRESS CATALOGING-IN-PUBLICATION DATA

Name: Mooney, Carla, 1970– author.
Title: Age Discrimination/by Carla Mooney.
Description: San Diego, CA: ReferencePoint Press, [2018] | Series:
  Discrimination in Society | Audience: Grade 9 to 12. | Includes
  bibliographical references and index.
Identifiers: LCCN 2018011692 (print) | LCCN 2018014828 (ebook) | ISBN
  9781682823804 (eBook) | ISBN 9781682823798 (hardback)
Subjects: LCSH: Age discrimination in employment—Juvenile literature. | Age
  discrimination in employment—Law and legislation—Juvenile literature.
Classification: LCC HD6279 (ebook) | LCC HD6279 .M66 2018 (print) | DDC
  331.3/981330973—dc23
LC record available at https://lccn.loc.gov/2018011692

CONTENTS

INTRODUCTION

Too Old to Work?

Forty-year-old Maria DeSimone applied for a job as a server at a Texas Roadhouse restaurant in Palm Bay, Florida, in 2009. DeSimone, a wife and mother, was looking to earn some extra income for her family. Because she had two years of restaurant work experience, she figured that she was a good fit for the job at Texas Roadhouse, a nationwide chain of casual steakhouses. She turned in her application, and the restaurant's manager said he would be in touch. When she did not hear from him, DeSimone called to follow up on the job. The manager informed her that the restaurant was no longer hiring. Later, she found out that a nineteen-year-old with no prior restaurant experience had gotten the job. In subsequent visits to the restaurant, DeSimone saw no one her age serving customers. "You're only going to see young people working there,"[1] she says.

DeSimone's experience at Texas Roadhouse was not unique, according to the US Equal Employment Opportunity Commission (EEOC). The EEOC is responsible for investigating charges of age discrimination and enforcing the 1967 Age Discrimination in Employment Act, which bans discrimination based on age. After its own investigation of hundreds of Texas Roadhouse restaurants across the country, the EEOC found a pattern of discrimination against job applicants age forty and over. The EEOC filed a lawsuit against the restaurant chain in federal court, which alleged that the company had discriminated against older job applicants by not hiring them for front-of-house jobs such as servers, bartenders, and hosts. DeSimone is one of fifty women and men named as claimants in the suit. In its lawsuit, the EEOC presented evidence of age discrimination, which included job applications on which management had posted yellow stickers with comments such as "Old 'N Chubby," "OLD," and "middle age . . . Doesn't really fit our image."[2] The EEOC also presented evidence showing that of the nearly two hundred thousand employees hired by Texas Roadhouse for front-of-house positions, fewer than three thousand were over forty years old. "We're thinking not just about the case at hand but also about influencing behavior more broadly," says Ray Peeler, a senior EEOC attorney-adviser. He cautions that employers cannot assume that older employees and job applicants do not have "the energy or excitement or whatever trait they're trying to capture."[3]

Texas Roadhouse denied the EEOC's allegations. It claimed to have hired thousands of older employees as servers, bartenders, and hosts. According to company spokesperson Travis Doster, the company does not ask job applicants their age. With more than 450 restaurants in the United States and thousands of employees, the company asserts its servers must be able to line dance, wear jeans, and work evenings and weekends. Even if these hiring criteria favor younger workers, the company argues it is legal because the requirements are job related and serve a business purpose. However, other legal experts, such as Carl Van Horn, a public policy professor at Rutgers University, are not so sure. "There are certainly older workers who can wear jeans and dance, so it's not a rational defense"[4] to not hire them, says Van Horn.

In 2017 the EEOC announced that Texas Roadhouse had settled the lawsuit. The company denied wrongdoing but agreed to pay $12 million in damages and to change its hiring and recruiting practices. "I am pleased to see this matter come to a mutually agreed-upon resolution," said EEOC acting chair Victoria Lipnic. "It is as important as ever to recognize the very real consequences of age discrimination and the need for job opportunities for older workers."[5]

> "It is as important as ever to recognize the very real consequences of age discrimination and the need for job opportunities for older workers."[5]
>
> —Victoria Lipnic, EEOC acting chair

When Does Age Matter?

In some jobs and careers, age matters. For example, National Football League players and other professional athletes need to be in peak physical condition, which typically occurs during their younger years. Firefighters and emergency workers must be able to move swiftly over uneven terrain and respond quickly to dangerous situations. Some jobs require workers to be able to lift heavy objects, see with twenty-twenty vision, or respond quickly to sounds. Other jobs require employees to have kept up with the latest training and industry practices. For these types of jobs, if prospective employees cannot physically perform the job or if their ideas or training are outdated, then they are simply not qualified for the job. If they are passed over for the position because they lack the necessary qualifications, it is not an example of age discrimination.

For the vast majority of jobs, however, age is not a factor. Instead, having certain skills, experience, a work ethic, and ideas are more important to be successful. An administrative assistant who is highly skilled in a variety of office technologies is a valuable asset, no matter if he or she is twenty-five or fifty-five years old. In these situations, applicants who have all of the necessary job qualifications, such as educational degrees, training, and technical skills, should have the opportunity to show what they can do. If they do not even get a callback and a chance because of their age, it is an example of age discrimination.

At age sixty-four, Jane had worked for more than a decade as a bartender for a local bar. When the bar was sold to new owners, the buyers told Jane that she was too old to be a bartender. They criticized her age and gender in front of customers and other bar employees. When the sale was final, the new owners fired Jane and replaced her with much younger female bartenders. Since then, Jane has filed a lawsuit alleging age and gender discrimination.

The restaurant industry has a demonstrated pattern of age discrimination. Lawsuits have been filed against restaurants for hiring only young people for front-of-house jobs such as servers, bartenders, and hosts.

An Overlooked Problem

Age discrimination is a pervasive problem in workplaces across the United States. According to the American Association of Retired Persons (AARP), a nonprofit organization that advocates for Americans aged fifty and older, two out of three workers between the ages of forty-five and seventy-four report that they have either seen or experienced age discrimination. Common though it may be, age discrimination often receives less attention than other forms of discrimination. "It could be that ageism versus other forms of discrimination is not taken as seriously or viewed as wrong as other types of discrimination, so we don't attack it with the same intensity,"[6] says Laurie McCann, a senior attorney at AARP Foundation Litigation. "I can make jokes about Dave's age and no one is going to get upset. If someone said something about race or gender there would be consequences, but it's OK to keep asking someone when they are going to retire to spend more time with their grandchildren,"[7] McCann says.

Age discrimination in the workplace occurs when employees and job applicants are not given the same opportunities as younger workers (or are treated differently) solely because of their age. Often age discrimination is based on the stereotype that older workers—because of their age—are unwilling or unable to learn new skills or perform certain tasks. Everyone ages differently. Many workers are capable of working in a job well into their seventies or longer. Age discrimination arises when employers assume that older workers cannot or will not do certain job tasks simply because of their age rather than evaluating each person on an individual basis.

Sometimes age discrimination can be direct, such as when an employer does not hire a qualified job applicant simply because of his or her age. Other times age discrimination is subtler, such as when an older employee is passed over for a promotion or a raise without an explanation. He or she may be given less-desirable work assignments or receive an unexplained poor performance review. In California, for example, firefighter George Corley sued the San Bernardino County Fire Protection District for age discrimination. He accused his employer of transferring older workers to farther-away assignments so that the long commute time might convince them to retire or quit. In 2011 then fifty-seven-year-old Corley was transferred to the county's North Desert division, an hour away from where he lived. When he did not retire, Corley was terminated in 2012 after thirty-eight years of service, including eight years as a division chief and battalion chief for San Bernardino County. During his employment, Corley was known as a good worker and had no record of disciplinary action. In 2016 a jury awarded Corley $704,000 in the lawsuit, ruling that age was a substantial and motivating reason for his firing.

Difficult to Prove

Although age discrimination is common in workplaces around the country, it can be difficult to prove. McCann explains that most employers "are smart enough not to make any sort of comment against the person's age, which would provide the smoking gun piece of evidence. So often, it's really not worth filing a job discrimination claim."[8]

Even so, age discrimination is a critical issue. Workers of all ages have contributions to make in every industry. Making employment decisions based on age—regardless of skills, qualifications, and experience—is inherently unfair. "The ability to find a new job should not be impeded because an employer considers someone the wrong age,"[9] says Kevin Berry, the New York district director of the EEOC.

"The ability to find a new job should not be impeded because an employer considers someone the wrong age."[9]

—Kevin Berry, EEOC New York district director

CHAPTER 1

How Serious A Problem Is Age Discrimination?

At age fifty-eight, Leslye Evans-Lane left her teaching job in New Mexico and moved to Oregon with her husband. As she settled into her new home and launched a job search, she never anticipated how difficult it would be to land a job. Over two years she submitted more than one hundred job applications. Eventually she was hired for a part-time academic job. However, when the job became full time six months later, she was replaced by a younger worker. "I applied for the full-time position and didn't even get an interview,"[10] says Evans-Lane. Evans-Lane believes that despite her experience and qualifications, her age made it more difficult to get hired and was the main reason why she was not considered for the full-time position.

Today the news is filled with stories about discrimination based on a person's gender, race, ethnicity, or sexual orientation. Although these forms of discrimination may grab the most headlines, age discrimination is one of the most common forms of discrimination in America's workplaces.

A Growing Problem in the Workplace

Age discrimination is a pervasive problem in the workplace, one that can take many forms. According to AARP, two-thirds of older workers have directly experienced or witnessed age discrimination at their workplace. According to an AARP survey, older workers reported experiencing several forms of age discrimination at work. They listed not being hired for a job for which they were qualified, not getting a promotion, and being laid off or fired—solely because of their age.

Hiring discrimination, or not being considered for a job despite having the necessary qualifications and experience, is one of the most common forms of age discrimination experienced by older Americans. According to research conducted by AARP in 2017, nearly two-thirds of workers aged fifty-five to sixty-four report that age is a barrier to getting hired. As an older job seeker, Philip ran into hiring discrimination during his recent job search. When speaking with a recruiter about a potential position, the recruiter "told me that his client looked at my resume and said it looked great, but then he found my LinkedIn profile and decided I'm a little long in the tooth for the job," says Philip. "The headhunter actually told me that the client said I was too old for the job. I asked him if that was illegal—I'm pretty sure it is—and he said that the client's view is that if they don't interview me, I'm not a candidate, so it's not discrimination."[11]

Claims of age discrimination in the workplace are rising. The EEOC received about one thousand claims of age-related discrimination in its first full year of enforcement in 1980. In 2016 the number of complaints reached more than twenty thousand.

Age discrimination is likely to become an even bigger problem as the American population and workforce ages. According to a 2016 report by the Population Reference Bureau, the number of Americans aged sixty-five and older is expected to increase from 46 million in 2016 to more than 98 million by 2060. In addition, many of these workers are delaying retirement and staying in the workplace longer, working into their seventies and even their eighties. By 2022, according to the US Census Bureau, 32 percent of people aged sixty-five to seventy-four will still be working. This is a significant increase from the 20 percent of the same age group working in 2002 and 27 percent in 2012.

The number of Americans aged sixty-five and older is expected to grow from 46 million in 2016 to 98 million by 2060. Many of these people are expected to continue working into their seventies and even eighties.

Older Americans are working longer because of a combination of factors, including longer life spans, better health, and the increased need for long-term financial security. "More and more older workers are out there wanting and needing to work,"[12] says Dan Kohrman, a senior attorney for AARP Foundation Litigation.

Too Expensive to Keep

Although many employers value experience, some have tried to cut costs by firing or laying off older workers. Experienced older workers often cost companies more money—in terms of salary and benefits. Some companies try to save money by replacing these older workers with lower-paid, younger workers.

At age fifty-seven, Marjorie Madfis was a New York–based digital marketing strategist and seventeen-year employee with IBM. In July 2013, Madfis and six other members of her nine-person team were laid off. The employees laid off were all women in their forties and fifties; the two team members who were retained were younger men who also happened to be earning less money. Madfis was surprised by the layoff. She had thought her career at IBM was on the rise. When she asked the company for a written explanation of the reasons for her termination, the company declined to do so. "They got rid of a group of highly skilled, highly effective, highly respected women, including me, for a reason nobody knows," says Madfis. "The only explanation is our age."[13]

In 2018 the nonprofit news organization ProPublica published its own investigation into IBM's hiring and firing practices. The organization's review, which spanned a five-year period, supports Madfis's claim. According to ProPublica, IBM eliminated more than twenty thousand employees aged forty and older during that five-year period. That number represents about 60 percent of the estimated total job cuts made by the company at its US offices during that period. ProPublica described a common scenario in which IBM appeared to lay off older workers and then rehire them as independent contractors. The change of status meant that they often performed the same job duties but at lower pay and without benefits. IBM did not respond directly to the news organization's findings. A company spokesperson noted, however, that IBM is proud of its ability (and the ability of its employees) to stay relevant in a changing business climate while always adhering to the law.

> "They got rid of a group of highly skilled, highly effective, highly respected women, including me, for a reason nobody knows. The only explanation is our age."[13]
>
> —Marjorie Madfis, a former IBM employee

Creating a Hostile Work Environment

Workplace discrimination does not always take the form of reduced job opportunities. Sometimes it involves a hostile work environment—one in which harassment based on age creates an uncomfortable or even abusive setting. Unwelcome and offensive conduct that targets someone based on age is a form of discrimination. Harassment can come from a supervisor, co-worker, client, or customer. Examples of age harassment include age-based jokes and comments; demeaning age-based cartoons, drawings, symbols, or gestures; and other verbal and physical behavior based on a person's age. For example, a co-worker may refer to an older employee as a *geezer* or make unwelcome jokes about receiving senior citizen discounts.

In some cases, unwelcome and harassing comments or incidents become so frequent or severe that they create a hostile work environment. Although some employees and bosses can make a workplace unpleasant, certain legal criteria must be met for a workplace to be considered hostile and unlawful. According to current EEOC guidelines, age harassment creates an unlawful, hostile work environment when a person must endure repeated offensive comments and conduct in order to keep their job and the offensive conduct is so severe or pervasive that it creates a work environment that any reasonable person would consider intimidating, hostile, or abusive.

Mandatory Retirement

For years, many companies enforced a mandatory retirement age for employees. A mandatory retirement policy forces employees to retire from their jobs when they hit a certain age, regardless of their desire or ability to work, their performance, or their financial situation. However, under the federal Age Discrimination in Employment Act of 1967, a mandatory retirement policy is a blatant form of age discrimination. Employers that force a person to retire based on his or her age can be sued in federal court. Only in certain limited situations are mandatory retirement policies acceptable. These include age sixty-five for commercial pilots or age fifty-five for publicly employed firefighters and law enforcement officers. Mandatory retirement at age sixty-five is also permitted in high-level positions such as CEOs who manage companies or subdivisions and direct the work of other employees.

Older workers can be harassed in the workplace. Younger supervisors or coworkers may target older workers with demeaning age-based jokes or refer to them with unkind names such as *geezers*.

At Montrose Memorial Hospital in Colorado, numerous staff alleged that they were victims of age discrimination. In a lawsuit against the hospital, a former nurse testified that comments by the hospital's chief nursing officer at the time were examples of the staff's discriminatory behavior toward older workers. The nurse said the supervisor commented, "We've got to get all of these old monkeys out of here and get cheery young things in."[14] Other managers and supervisors also made ageist comments, saying they preferred younger and fresher nurses. "Managers made it evident that they preferred to socialize with younger employees. They perpetuated a culture where older employees felt disregarded and ignored,"[15] says Laurie Jaeckel, a trial attorney at the EEOC's Denver office. After several former employees alleged that they were forced to resign or retire, the EEOC launched an investigation. In 2018 the EEOC announced that it had reached a settlement with the hospital. Although the hospital did not acknowledge that it had discriminated against older employees, it agreed to pay $400,000 to twenty-nine former employees.

Placing a High Value on Youth

For industries that place a high value on youth, such as fashion, technology, and advertising, age discrimination is even more rampant. Fifty-nine-year-old Pete Denes had years of experience in the tech industry running a $200 million sales division at the consumer electronics company Hitachi. Yet after he left that job, he struggled for years to find another job in tech, traveling from California to Arizona and eventually Nebraska. After nearly a decade and hundreds of rejected résumés, Denes now believes that it is "virtually impossible to get my foot in the door anywhere."[16] Today he sells yard and monument signs in Omaha.

The tech industry is well known for being filled with young employees in their twenties and thirties. According to the research firm PayScale, the median age of an American worker was forty-two in 2016. At social media giant Facebook, the median age was twenty-nine. At Google, it was thirty; at Amazon, thirty; at Apple, thirty-one; and at Microsoft, thirty-three. According to one expert, tech companies can view people as young as thirty-five as out of touch and stodgy. "Ageism is very real, especially in start-ups where being older is seen as a liability," says forty-five-year-old Aileen Gemma Smith, the chief executive officer (CEO) of Vizalytics, a tech start-up in New York. "It assumes you won't work hard, long hours, and have out-of-date skills. I have certainly experienced investors in New York and Silicon Valley who looked down on myself and co-founder (chief technology officer Chris Smith is 55) for not being 'young' enough to innovate."[17] In addition, some tech employers worry that older

> "Ageism is very real, especially in start-ups where being older is seen as a liability."[17]
>
> —Aileen Gemma Smith, the CEO of Vizalytics, a tech start-up in New York

Age Discrimination at Google

Workers in the tech industry have long asserted that the industry heavily favors youth. One of the industry's giants, Google, faces a class-action lawsuit, alleging that the company engaged in age discrimination. As of 2017, more than 250 people have joined the class-action lawsuit. One of the plaintiffs, Cheryl Fillekes, is a systems engineer who alleges that between 2007 and 2014 Google passed her over for several engineering positions for which she was qualified because of her age. In court documents, Fillekes says that a Google recruiter told her to put her college graduation dates on her résumé so that Google interviewers could see how old she was. Google spokespersons have denied the allegations, asserting that the company has strong policies in place to prevent any form of discrimination in the workplace, including that based on age.

employees might not have as much time to devote to work as younger employees have. "In tech, they need people willing to work 16 hours a day, without overtime," says Javier, a thirtysomething tech professional. "Someone with a family is not going to be able to dedicate that much time to their job."[18] The claims are backed up by a 2017 survey of US tech workers by Indeed.com, which found that 43 percent of workers feared they would lose their job because of their age.

A bias toward youth can also be found in the advertising industry, where some say the average age of workers is around twenty-seven. Industry insiders say that some agencies push out employees when they reach age fifty or fifty-five. "Age discrimination is rife against both genders,"[19] says one former, unnamed agency employee.

The perception that older workers cannot work with digital media may be one factor in advertising's age bias. While in his midfifties, John Grenier-Ferris embarked on the search for a new job. He was asked at an ad agency job interview where he learned how to use social media. The interviewer appeared to be surprised that someone of Grenier-Ferris's age could successfully master social media. "It was as if someone was asking me 'where did you learn brain surgery?'" he says. "Social media is not that hard to figure out."[20] Jay Haines, the founder of executive search firm Grace Blue, agrees that the advertising industry values youth when looking to hire new employees. "Singly, the most undervalued commodity in this business is experience. It's overlooked in favor of the bright shiny object," he says. Anyone who is fifty or older is often overlooked, regardless of their experience and skills. "I see an unconscious bias to hire the young gun or the up-and-comer all the time,"[21] says Haines.

Increasing Evidence of Discrimination

When older workers have trouble getting hired or even getting an interview for a job for which they are qualified, many suspect age discrimination is a factor. In 2015 the Federal Reserve Bank of San Francisco conducted a nationwide field test to determine if employers were favoring younger job applicants over older ones. In the study, researchers created résumés for fake job applicants. Each fake applicant had identical skills and qualifications, but they were divided into three groups based on these age ranges: twenty-nine to thirty-one, forty-nine to fifty-one, and sixty-four to sixty-six. The researchers submitted the résumés to open positions for administrative assistant, retail sales, janitorial, and security jobs. They chose these fields because each employs large numbers of low-skilled workers with a wide range of ages. In addition, the researchers believed that because employers in these fields saw large numbers of workers and applications, they would be less familiar with individual applicants and less likely to figure out the résumés were fake. "We chose fields that are pretty big and tend to have large numbers of older workers,"[22] says David Neumark, an economics professor at the University of California, Irvine, and the coauthor of the study.

Older workers often get discouraged when they fail to get a callback or even an initial interview for a job for which they are qualified. Research has shown that age discrimination is a significant factor in the job market.

In total, the researchers submitted fake résumés for forty thousand job applicants to thousands of real positions in twelve cities. All résumés submitted for a particular job were identical except for the applicant's age. In all areas, the researchers found that the young and middle-aged applicants were called back for interviews at a higher rate than the older group, a finding the study's authors say is consistent with age discrimination in hiring. "The call-back rate—the rate by which employers contact us and say we'd like to interview you—drops from young applicants to middle-aged applicants and drops further from middle-aged applicants to older applicants,"[23] Neumark says.

The researchers also found a sharper drop-off in callback rates for older women than for older men. According to Neumark, this can be a serious problem for older women. "Already many women outlive their husbands and end up quite poor. . . . If women worked until they were older, their post-retirement financial straits might be eased—but our study indicates that right now many of them don't get that option."[24] says Neumark.

As the number of older workers grows, the challenges they and their companies face will also increase. Companies must figure out how to create a welcoming workplace for workers of all ages and take advantage of the skills and experiences older workers bring to the job. If not handled correctly, issues can arise that can have a negative impact on the organization. "This is all new. There is no universal approach," says Robert Preziosi, a professor of organizational studies and human resources at Nova Southeastern University in Florida. "We are seeing a potpourri of approaches driven by what individual companies think will work best for them in terms of their bottom line."[25]

CHAPTER 2

How Are People Hurt by Age Discrimination?

For many years, Claudette Lindsey worked as a teacher and a family support specialist with the Head Start schools in Park Forest, Illinois. Then she was laid off in 2013. Even with her years of experience and a bachelor's degree in early childhood education, Lindsey, who is in her early sixties, could not find a new job. After job hunting unsuccessfully, Lindsey has been volunteering and going to a weekly workshop for seniors, where she practices interviewing and polishes her résumé. Although she has not landed a job yet, she is determined to keep trying. Still, she recognizes that her age is a barrier to getting hired. "I'm a more mature worker," she says. "You know that an employer might go with someone younger." Lindsey hopes that her volunteer work with teens at her church will lead to a job at a local high school. She wishes that employers would put more value on the skills and experience older workers can bring to a business and the benefits of having a workplace with people from different generations. "I wish companies would look at having an intergenerational workplace," she says. "The seasoned workers . . . have a lot of enthusiasm. We have a lot of lives in us."[26]

> "I wish companies would look at having an intergenerational workplace. The seasoned workers . . . have a lot of enthusiasm. We have a lot of lives in us."[26]
>
> —Claudette Lindsey, a worker in her early sixties

Discrimination Impacts
Ability to Earn a Living

Today people are living longer, healthier lives than ever before. As a result, many people are working longer as well. According to the US Bureau of Labor Statistics, about 20 percent of Americans aged sixty-five and older are working. Workers in their fifties, sixties, and seventies often have many productive work years left in them. These workers still need to earn an income to pay for houses, cars, food, kids in college, vacations, and more. "In my research, the first thing I hear from older workers looking for a job is that they need to work," says Ofer Sharone, an assistant professor at the Sloan School of Management at the Massachusetts Institute of Technology (MIT). "They may be over 60 and very close to traditional retirement age, but they feel they don't have the resources to retire. And many are feeling healthy. They're at the top of their game and wanting to make a contribution,"[27] says Sharone.

> "Older workers . . . may be over 60 and very close to traditional retirement age, but they feel they don't have the resources to retire."[27]
>
> —Ofer Sharone, an assistant professor at the MIT Sloan School of Management

When they are prevented from doing that solely because of their age, it hurts. It hurts financially, and it hurts emotionally. Ron Di Giorgio, age fifty-two, worked for more than thirty years as a maintenance electrician. When the last project he was working on was canceled, all the contractors on the job, including Di Giorgio, were let go. Since then, he has struggled to find work. "It's not for a lack of trying," says Di Giorgio. He estimates that he has sent out more than 250 résumés in the past year. "I started off really pushing for work but after eight or nine months of doing that, I was over it. I'm just sick and tired of doing it, because there's no one out there who wants you. I haven't had one call back. It's depressing. It gets to you." Di Giorgio believes that his age puts him at a disadvantage looking for work. When he was in his twenties and thirties, he could find work easily. Now, he cannot even get a callback. Even when he applied for a construction job at a residential building site, the employer said he did not have enough experience. "What experience do you need to shovel a bit of dirt, really? They look at the fact I'm 52 years old. They want young blokes who are fit, who will break their backs for them. Maybe I won't. They don't know you until you work for them, until they give you an opportunity,"[28] he says.

The months without a steady income have taken a toll on Di Giorgio's financial situation. For years, Di Giorgio has been a collector of a variety of items, from samurai swords to vintage children's toys. Now, he has been forced to sell some of his collectibles for money to pay some of his living expenses. Di Giorgio

Approximately 20 percent of Americans aged sixty-five and older are working. Workers in their sixties and seventies often have many productive work years ahead of them.

also has two daughters, ages eighteen and twenty-two, who occasionally need his support as they go to school and begin their careers. "They still need money, they still need help. You don't lose that responsibility. That's another stress that goes onto you, you sort of feel like you're not doing your job, by not looking after them," he says. If given the chance, Di Giorgio says he would be happy to work another twenty years or more. "It's a joke, talking about retiring people at 68 to 70 years old. That's wonderful if you've got a job that'll take you there. But most people won't have a job that will make it that far."[29]

The Impact on Retirement

Age discrimination can also affect a worker's ability to save for and fund retirement. Many older workers have specific plans about how and when they will transition into retirement and the money they plan to earn and save in order to build a sufficient retirement fund. According to a 2017 survey of workers by the Transamerica Center for Retirement Studies, about 67 percent of baby boomers (individuals born between 1946 and 1964) plan to work (or are

Hurting Companies

Not only does age discrimination hurt older workers, but it can also harm companies. It exposes a company to legal claims and negatively impacts worker productivity and performance. When age discrimination forces older employees out of the workforce, companies lose years of valuable work experience that could be put to good use for the business. Age discrimination is often noticed by many employees, even those who do not directly experience it. This can create a negative environment with poor morale for all workers, which can negatively impact worker productivity. In fact, workers may become concerned that they could also be discriminated against as they age. These fears could have the unintended consequence of causing productive employees to leave the company, not because they are targets of age discrimination but because they fear they could be in the future.

already working) past age sixty-five or do not plan to retire at all. Fifty-four percent plan to work after they retire, often citing financial and healthy aging reasons. Twenty percent of boomers plan to work as long as they can in their current position. Other boomers (45 percent) plan a gradual transition into retirement, during which they expect to work less hours and enjoy more leisure time or take on a less demanding role.

As they age, however, many older workers find they have little control over how long they will work. They may encounter an economic downturn that causes employers to reduce staff, or they may experience physical and health constraints that limit their ability to work. Likewise, an employer might encourage older employees to take early retirement. According to research by the Employee Benefit Research Institute, nearly 50 percent of current retirees retired earlier than they had planned. In addition, about 60 percent of older workers who are let go involuntarily end up retiring early, according to the Center for Retirement Research at Boston College. Once they are out of work, older workers face steep challenges in finding new jobs.

When this happens, retirement savings are among the first things to suffer. When workers lose income during the decade leading up to retirement, it reduces the credits used to calculate future Social Security benefits. Lost income can also cause older workers to file for Social Security benefits early, which significantly reduces their lifetime benefits. When income from a job stops, older workers are no longer able to contribute to retirement savings, leaving them short of their goals. In many cases, they are forced to spend some of their retirement savings early to pay for daily living expenses.

Lower Pay and Long-Term Unemployment

Because many companies refuse to hire older workers, even if they have the skills required for the job, some of those workers end up taking low-skill, low-paying jobs. These workers are underemployed, working in jobs below their education or skill levels or that offer fewer hours than they want to work. Underemployed workers earn less income, leaving little for retirement and other savings. Society also suffers when older workers are underemployed. With less disposable income, workers often spend less and are at greater risk of poverty, which affects businesses and communities. In addition, many of these low-skill jobs are typically first jobs for teens. When the jobs are filled by older workers, teens miss out on the opportunity to join the workforce and gain valuable work experience.

In the search for a suitable job, older workers are more likely to be unemployed for longer periods of time than their younger counterparts. Long-term unemployment is defined as being jobless for twenty-seven weeks or longer. According to a 2015 report by the Bureau of Labor Statistics, long-term unemployment increases with age. In 2014, 45 percent of workers aged fifty-five and older were unemployed for twenty-seven weeks or longer, as compared to only 22 percent of the unemployed under age twenty-five and 36 percent for those between the ages of twenty-five and fifty-four.

The longer older workers are out of the workforce, the more likely they will be to stop looking for work entirely and leave the workforce for good. According to a 2013 Urban Institute study, half of unemployed workers over age sixty-two drop out of the labor force within nine months of being unemployed. Although many of these workers are not considered part of the official US labor force, many would prefer to return to work if they were given an opportunity. Out of the workforce, these workers are forced to dip into retirement savings or file for Social Security benefits early, reducing their lifetime benefits and weakening their long-term financial stability.

In addition to affecting a person's financial stability, long-term unemployment can have a negative effect on the health of older workers, particularly those who experience unemployment in their late fifties or early sixties. When faced with a period of long-term unemployment or even unwilling retirement, many of these workers lose employer-provided health insurance, often at a time

Many Workers Expect to Be Working Past Age Sixty-Five

More than half of workers polled in a 2017 survey said that they expected to be working past the age of sixty-five, or do not plan to retire at all. However, ideas about working in later life are not the same for all age groups. Most baby boomers, for instance, said they expect to work past age sixty-five or do not plan to retire while only 41 percent of millennials said they plan to be working that long.

At What Age Do You Expect to Retire?

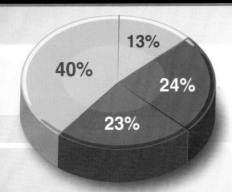

All Workers (%)

NET–After Age 65 or Do Not Plan to Retire = 53%

Workers by Generation (%)

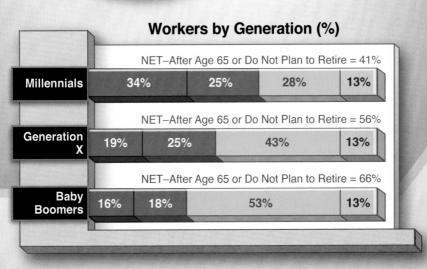

Millennials
NET–After Age 65 or Do Not Plan to Retire = 41%
34% | 25% | 28% | 13%

Generation X
NET–After Age 65 or Do Not Plan to Retire = 56%
19% | 25% | 43% | 13%

Baby Boomers
NET–After Age 65 or Do Not Plan to Retire = 66%
16% | 18% | 53% | 13%

Before Age 65   At Age 65   After Age 65   Do Not Plan to Retire

Note: Baby boomers are usually identified as people who were born between 1946 and 1964. Generation X is usually identified as individuals who were born between 1965 and 1980. Millennials are usually identified as people who were born between 1981 and 1996.

Source: Transamerica Center for Retirement Studies, "Wishful Thinking or Within Reach? Three Generations Prepare for 'Retirement,'" December 2017. www.transamericacenter.org.

in their lives when they need it most. Some choose to purchase individual health insurance policies, which can be very expensive. Others forgo insurance entirely, paying for health services as they use them until they reach age sixty-five and qualify for Medicare. Without insurance, many reduce the amount of health care they use. This can lead to a significant health risk for people who may already be experiencing chronic health problems and are more likely to experience significant events such as heart attacks or cancer diagnoses.

Women Are Hurt More by Age Discrimination

Although many older workers are impacted by age discrimination, women may feel its effects even more strongly than men. Based on the results of the San Francisco Federal Reserve Bank's 2015 age discrimination field experiment, the résumés of older women get significantly fewer callbacks than those of older men and of younger male and female job applicants. The researchers are not sure why this difference occurred in their experiment, but they suggest two general reasons why older women might suffer more from age discrimination. First, age discrimination laws may do

A Shortage of Skilled Workers

Across the country, businesses are having a hard time finding and retaining skilled workers. A 2017 survey of small business owners by US Bank found that 61 percent said they are having extreme or moderate difficulty finding quality, skilled employees needed to grow their businesses. The shortage is greater in rural areas, but it is also a problem in cities. In manufacturing, health care, retail, hospitality, tech, construction, and more, employers are losing out on business because they cannot find the workers they need. As a result, many have had to pay more to attract and retain desired workers. Some people believe that the shortage of skilled workers could be reduced by an overlooked segment of the workforce—older, experienced workers.

According to a 2015 study, résumés of older women get significantly fewer callbacks than those of older men. Experts suggest this is partly due to older women suffering from both age and gender discrimination.

less to protect older women who might experience both age and gender discrimination. In addition, older female workers may be at a greater disadvantage in hiring. "Evidence suggests that physical appearance matters more for women" than men in the work world, the researchers say. They add that, in the view of hiring managers, "age detracts more from physical appearance for women than for men."[30] While the study tracked callbacks based only on résumés, the researchers suggest that employers could have used age to estimate a candidate's attractiveness, especially when hiring for jobs that require a lot of interaction with customers, such as sales positions.

Fifty-five-year-old Laura Milvy does not mind getting older, and she accepts her wrinkled skin and graying hair. Yet she suspects that her age, along with her gender, have made it harder for her to find a job. Milvy spent a year unemployed and job hunting until she was hired for her current position as an assistant to the CEO at the Commonwealth Club in San Francisco. Although she cannot say for sure that her callback rate from potential employers was less than younger job applicants, she believes that she was less likely to be hired for jobs after in-person interviews. "There needs to be more awareness that when you reach 50, you don't need to be put out to pasture,"[31] says Milvy.

> "There needs to be more awareness that when you reach 50, you don't need to be put out to pasture."[31]
>
> —Laura Milvy, age fifty-five

As women typically live longer than men, they could benefit more from working longer. Letting older women go out of the workforce or forcing them into lower-paying jobs simply because of their age can significantly affect their ability to earn a living and save for and fund their retirement. As a result, the reduced income can have a big impact on their quality of life now and in the future.

Serious Consequences

Age discrimination can have serious, long-lasting consequences on older workers now and in the future. Without a job or one that pays a decent salary, older workers struggle to pay for the expenses of everyday life, from mortgages and car payments to college tuition and groceries. To make ends meet, many are forced to sacrifice their future retirement, skimping on retirement savings, taking funds out of retirement accounts, or accessing federal Social Security benefits earlier than anticipated. For women, the consequences can be even more severe, as they are more likely to experience age discrimination than their male peers and are also more likely to live longer and need a reliable income stream now and in the future.

CHAPTER 3

How Does the Law Address Age Discrimination?

For more than four decades, Donetta Raymond worked in manufacturing. Right out of high school, she followed her father's footsteps into a manufacturing job because it paid well in her hometown of Wichita, Kansas. Raymond started working as a sheet metal mechanic and found no shortage of work in Wichita, where several large aircraft manufacturers had plants. Over time, Raymond learned new skills and advanced to become a production operation specialist on 737 airplane fuselages for Boeing and later Spirit AeroSystems. Over the years, she consistently earned good reviews from her supervisors, including an "A" rating in 2012 from Spirit AeroSystems. The following year, management conducted a separate review. This time, Raymond was given a "C" rating. And only a few months later, the company laid off hundreds of workers, including fifty-nine-year-old Raymond.

Spirit AeroSystems claimed the layoffs of 360 salaried employees and managers was necessary for the company to stay competitive. However, workers discovered that nearly half of those laid off were age forty or older. They filed a complaint with the EEOC, which found that they had a valid claim of age discrimination. Then, in 2017, seventy former employees, including Raymond, filed an age discrimination lawsuit in the federal district court in Wichita. In addition to claiming that they were targeted because they were age forty or older, the workers allege that they were chosen for termination because they or their spouse had serious medical conditions that could potentially increase the cost of the company's health insurance coverage. Spirit denies that it discriminated against the older employees when making the termination decision. "Reductions in force are never easy, however all decisions are based on job-related, nondiscriminatory criteria," says Fred Malley, Spirit's spokesman. "We are confident the evidence in this case will show Spirit is compliant with the law in its employment practices."[32]

Age discrimination cases like this one are becoming more common across the United States. When workers believe they have been discriminated against because of their age, they can file a discrimination complaint with the EEOC. In 2016, nearly twenty-one thousand age discrimination complaints were filed. "Once layoffs were done by reverse seniority. It was last in, first out, so the more senior workers kept their jobs," says Robert J. Gordon, an economics professor at Northwestern University, who studies the country's growth and workforce productivity. "Now we're seeing a transition from the age of favoritism to that of age

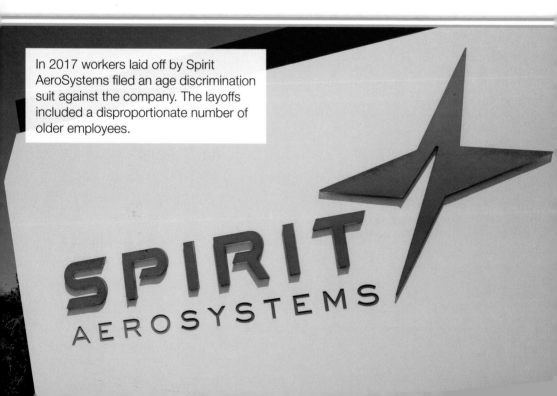

In 2017 workers laid off by Spirit AeroSystems filed an age discrimination suit against the company. The layoffs included a disproportionate number of older employees.

SPIRIT
AEROSYSTEMS

discrimination, because newer workers are allowed to stay on while more costly, older workers are let go."[33]

The Age Discrimination in Employment Act

One of the main tools used to fight age discrimination is the Age Discrimination in Employment Act (ADEA) of 1967. This law came about as a result of a gap in the Civil Rights Act, passed by Congress in 1964. Under Title VII of the Civil Rights Act, discrimination based on race, color, religion, sex, or national origin is prohibited.

At the time, Congress elected to exclude age as one of the protected classes under Title VII. However, Congress directed the secretary of labor to report on age discrimination. The report, presented in 1967 to Congress, showed that many older Americans were being excluded from or driven out of the workforce, and the problem was getting worse. Workers aged forty to forty-five were more likely than younger workers to be fired or laid off. Once unemployed, they encountered significant difficulty finding new work, and many eventually became so discouraged that they stopped job hunting. In addition, in an age before the Internet, older workers had few resources to help them find a job; established employment services were no help. In addition, the report informed Congress that age discrimination was regulated at the state level by a variety of laws that lacked any consistency. Whereas some states appeared to have effective age discrimination laws, others were deemed to be ineffective. The difference in laws from state to state caused confusion, especially among businesses that operated in multiple states or had employees who traveled from state to state. The report's findings motivated Congress to take action.

> "Once layoffs were done by reverse seniority. . . . Now we're seeing a transition from the age of favoritism to that of age discrimination, because newer workers are allowed to stay on while more costly, older workers are let go."[33]
>
> —Robert J. Gordon, an economics professor at Northwestern University

The majority of lawmakers agreed that something needed to be done to stop age discrimination in America. Senator Stephen Young of Ohio was among those who favored passage of a law that would protect people from age discrimination. A member of the Senate's Special Committee on Aging, he stated,

> The view that a man or woman is so old at 65 as to warrant compulsory retirement from industry stems from an era before the turn of the century and comes to us from a period when life expectancy was about half of the life expectancy of Americans and Europeans at the present time. . . . In fact, today [people] are not as old at 65 [in] thought, action, physical and mental ability as men and women . . . were at the age of 40 in the 1880's. Yet, for some reason or other, we Americans have adhered to this view of 65 as being the proper age for retirement notwithstanding the fact that this concept is today as outdated as are flint-lock muskets and candle dips of the eighteenth century.[34]

Congress passed the ADEA in December 1967, and it was signed into law by President Lyndon B. Johnson that month.

Exceptions to the ADEA

There are several situations in which the ADEA does not apply. For example, companies that have less than twenty employees are not covered by the act. Additionally, executives or others in high policy-making positions may be required to retire at age sixty-five if they receive annual retirement pension benefits of at least $44,000. The ADEA also does not apply in certain situations when age is an essential part of the job—known as bona fide occupational qualification. For example, when a company wants to hire an actor to play the role of a fifteen-year-old or a teen clothing store hires models for a new advertising campaign, the ability to appear young is a required part of the job.

In December 1967, President Lyndon Johnson signed into law the ADEA. The law came about because of a gap in the Civil Rights Act of 1964, which did not include a provision for age discrimination.

Not everyone supported the ADEA. Many trade associations opposed the legislation, believing it was not a matter that needed to be mandated by law. For example, the National Association of Manufacturers argued that employer efforts to combat unemployment of older workers should be voluntary, not mandated by law. In addition, the Chamber of Commerce, while applauding ADEA's goal of antidiscrimination, also opposed the law.

What Does the ADEA Do?

The ADEA is the main federal law that bans employment-related age discrimination. The ADEA applies to companies with more than twenty employees but excludes elected officials, military personnel, and independent contractors. It offers protection to employees age forty or older against age discrimination in all areas of employment, including hiring, firing, pay, promotions, layoffs, job responsibilities, benefits, and training. The ADEA states that it is illegal for an employer

1. to fail or refuse to hire or to discharge any individual or otherwise discriminate against any individual with respect to his compensation, terms, conditions, or privileges of employment, because of such individual's age;

2. to limit, segregate, or classify his employees in any way which would deprive or tend to deprive any individual of employment opportunities or otherwise adversely affect his status as an employee, because of such individual's age; or

3. to reduce the wage rate of any employee in order to comply with this chapter [of federal law].[35]

It also prohibits age discrimination by employment agencies, barring them from refusing to refer job applicants to hiring companies because of their age. In addition, the ADEA bans employers from listing age requirements in job ads or asking questions related to age during hiring interviews.

American workers were quick to embrace their rights under the ADEA. In 1980, the first full year in which the EEOC enforced the ADEA, nearly 20 percent of all discrimination complaints filed with the commission involved age discrimination. By 1986 the percentage of age-related claims handled by the EEOC rose to 25 percent. As of 2017, nearly 22 percent of EEOC claims involved age discrimination.

Not all of these claims become lawsuits, but some do. In one example, the EEOC filed a lawsuit against Hawaii HealthCare Professionals, a Honolulu-based home health care services company, in 2010. According to the lawsuit, the company's owner ordered the firing of Debra Moreno, a fifty-four-year-old office coordinator. The firing was done in spite of reports by the office manager, who had hired and supervised Moreno, that she was a competent and efficient worker. The owner allegedly told the office manager that Moreno "looks old," "sounds old on the telephone," and is "like a bag of bones."[36] The owner also allegedly stated that Moreno was not the type of person she wanted to represent the company. After learning about the owner's comments, Moreno filed a discrimination complaint with the EEOC. "When I learned that my age was the reason for the disparaging remarks and termination, I was embarrassed and demoralized. For me, it was the ultimate blow. Age had never before been a consideration for me,"[37] says Moreno.

After investigating Moreno's claim, the EEOC filed a federal lawsuit against the company and its owner. The agency characterized the owner's behavior as a form of age discrimination and stated that it violated the ADEA. After reviewing the evidence, in 2012 the court ordered the company to pay Moreno $190,000 in damages. It also ordered the company to develop and implement procedures to prevent future age discrimination and train staff and supervisors about their rights regarding age discrimination. "Age should never be a factor when evaluating an employee or job applicant's worth. What makes this case especially appalling is the flagrant disregard for a worker's abilities, coupled with disparaging ageist remarks and thinking. The EEOC will not tolerate such violations of civil rights law and is pleased by the court's decision,"[38] says Anna Y. Park, a regional attorney for the EEOC's Los Angeles district office, which oversees the agency's litigation in Hawaii.

> "When I learned that my age was the reason for the disparaging remarks and termination, I was embarrassed and demoralized. For me, it was the ultimate blow. Age had never before been a consideration for me."[37]
>
> —Debra Moreno, age fifty-four

Banning Age-Related Harassment

The ADEA also prohibits age-related workplace harassment and bans employers from punishing workers who report this type of behavior or any other acts of age discrimination. Under the ADEA, harassment is more than a disparaging comment or two; it is defined as a pattern of behavior that creates a hostile work environment. This was a factor in an EEOC lawsuit against Advance Components, a Texas distributor of specialty fasteners. The suit alleged that the company's executive vice president, Gary Craven, made ageist comments to employee Dan Miller, a sixty-four-year-old national sales manager. According to the lawsuit, Craven called Miller "old-fashioned" and repeatedly stated his desire to hire younger salesmen, stating "30-30-30. Hire a 30-year-old with an IQ of 30 and pay him $30,000." Craven also allegedly talked about preferring young salespeople because he believed them to be more "driven" and that he wanted to "put young guys on the street."[39] Eventually Craven fired Miller and hired a replacement in his thirties the next day.

> **"Older workers have the right to be evaluated based on their abilities and not based on their age."[40]**
>
> —Attorney William C. Backhaus of the EEOC

In a settlement of the lawsuit in 2012, Advance Components agreed to pay $201,000 to Miller, although the company did not admit any wrongdoing. It also agreed to train management on age discrimination policies and procedures and enforce a written policy against age discrimination and retaliation. "Older workers have the right to be evaluated based on their abilities and not based on their age," says EEOC senior trial attorney William C. Backhaus. "Every employer, large and small, needs to recognize the importance of avoiding stereotypes, including those about age and older workers. Advance Components wrongly assumed that Mr. Miller's age, 64, interfered with his ability to connect with customers. It didn't—we learned that he was their top producer and that customers loved him."[40]

The Older Workers Benefit Protection Act

Although the ADEA offered many important protections for older workers, it did not cover all situations involving age discrimination. In 1989 the US Supreme Court ruled in *Public Employee*

Retirement System of Ohio v. Betts that employee benefits plans are not protected by the ADEA. As a result, an employer could deny or reduce benefits received by older workers as long as the employee's wages were not affected. An employer might do this in hopes of saving the company money. The cost of group health insurance plans, for instance, may be affected by the age of workers. Businesses with older workers might pay more for these plans than businesses with younger workers. All benefits, including disability, health insurance, life insurance, and pensions, were deemed to be outside the reach of the ADEA and age discrimination claims.

In response to this case, Congress passed an amendment to the ADEA, the Older Workers Benefit Protection Act (OWBPA) of 1990. The OWBPA amended the original law, making it illegal to refuse to provide benefits to older employees, reducing their benefits, or firing them in order to avoid paying benefits. The OWBPA covers life and health insurance, disability and retirement benefits,

The ADEA was amended in 1990 to include protection of health care benefits for older workers. The amendment states that health benefits must be equal for all employees, regardless of age.

and pensions. It states that all benefits must be equal for all workers, regardless of age.

The OWBPA does recognize that some benefits cost more to provide as employees age. Under the OWBPA, employers must offer older workers benefits that cost the employer the same amounts as benefits provided to younger workers. For example, the cost of life insurance is always higher for an older person than it is for a younger one. Under the law, an employer would provide a $50,000 policy for an older worker and a $75,000 policy for a younger worker as long as the cost to the employer is the same for both policies. For benefits that do not increase in cost with age, such as severance pay, vacation time, or a 401(k) matching program, employers must provide the same benefits to all workers, regardless of age.

State and Local Laws

In addition to federal age discrimination laws, almost every state has its own laws that prohibit age discrimination in employment. In some cases, local municipalities have adopted their own laws too. In many cases, state and local laws provide greater protections to older workers than federal laws. For example, the ADEA only applies to workers age forty and older. Yet many employees claim that age discrimination can begin even when a worker is in his or her thirties. Several states, including Hawaii and Maryland, provide age discrimination protection to workers before age forty.

Many state laws also apply to more businesses than do federal laws. Whereas the federal ADEA, for instance, only applies to employers with twenty employees or more, many state laws cover businesses with fewer employees. For example, in California the Fair Housing and Employment Act applies to employers with as few as five workers. Age discrimination laws in several other states (including Colorado, Arizona, and Michigan) apply to all businesses regardless of size or number of employees.

Proving Age Discrimination

Although age discrimination is prohibited by a variety of laws at various levels, many incidents are never reported. One reason for this, experts say, is the difficulty of proving bias. To prove an age discrimination claim, an employee must show that age was a determining factor in an employer's adverse employment action. But biased views and actions are not always explicit. According to Laurie McCann, a senior attorney with AARP, most employers know they should not comment on someone's age. Without that direct evidence of discrimination, many employees choose not to file a job discrimination claim because they believe it will be too difficult to prove. In addition, proving age discrimination in hiring against a *potential* employer can be even more difficult. "Unless the older person knows who was hired and can compare their qualifications, then all they have is a hunch and a gut feeling,"[41] McCann says.

This is exactly what happened to Tina Marshall after she was laid off in 2014. At first Marshall believed she would easily find a new job. She had a bachelor's degree with a recent graduation date and good work experience in manufacturing sales and operations. She submitted her résumé and had no problem getting called back for job interviews. Phone interviews often went well, but when she arrived on-site for a face-to-face interview, it became clear to Marshall, then sixty, that the hiring managers were expecting someone much younger. She felt there was little she could do about it, however. No one actually said anything inappropriate. Marshall admits that she has become very conscious about her age and worries "that my resume has been singled out and stamped as 'OLD' and I will never get another chance at anything again." Even so, she does not plan to file an age discrimination claim against the potential employers. "It's too hard to prove," she says. "It always seems that companies leave just enough older people in place to at least make it appear they are not being discriminating."[42] Instead, Marshall plans to sell her house to reduce expenses and look for a part-time job.

In 2009 the Supreme Court's ruling in *Gross v. FBL Financial* made it even more difficult for workers to prove age discrimination. In the case, insurance executive Jack Gross was one of a dozen employees demoted at FBL Financial. All were high performers at the company, but they also were older workers. Gross, who was fifty-four years old at the time, sued for age discrimination. He presented evidence that his demotion was based in part on his age. For its part, FBL claimed that its actions to demote workers, including Gross, were part of a corporate restructuring plan. Although Gross initially prevailed in lower courts, the Supreme Court overturned the lower courts' verdict. The court ruled that the employee must prove that age was the main reason for discrimination. Before *Gross*, if an employer had a business reason for firing or demoting an employee but also based the action

Evidence of Age Discrimination

Claims of age discrimination are often difficult to prove legally. Simply being replaced by a younger worker or a company hiring a younger applicant is generally not enough to prove a claim of age discrimination. Often people who experience this form of discrimination have a feeling instead of direct proof that they are being targeted because of their age. If a person believes he or she is the victim of discrimination based on age, the following actions can be used as evidence:

- Frequent comments made by managers and coworkers about the person's age.
- Managers give unexplained, declining performance reviews as the employee ages.
- Supervisors and human resources discipline older workers for behavior that they disregard in younger employees.
- Management hires and promotes younger employees more frequently than older workers.
- Management assigns unpleasant tasks to older workers while younger employees get more attractive assignments.

on age, the employee had a valid age discrimination claim. After *Gross*, employees must show that age discrimination was the main factor in the employer's action. Under this ruling, workers claiming age discrimination now have a higher burden of proof under the ADEA than they did for claims of other forms of discrimination under the Civil Rights Act's Title VII.

Against the Law but Difficult to Prove

Laws like the ADEA have given workers protections against age discrimination in the workplace. These laws have made it possible for workers to file complaints with the EEOC and take employers to court for age-related termination, harassment, and other forms of age bias. In some cases, the workers have prevailed and have been awarded significant monetary damages. However, while these laws provide added protection for older workers, they have not actually eliminated age discrimination in the workplace. Incidents of age bias in all aspects of the employment process still happen. When they do, it is often difficult to prove age discrimination in court. According to Michael Harper of the Boston University School of Law, the ADEA is not nearly as effective as Title VII, which bans employment discrimination based on race, color, religion, gender, and national origin. "For no good policy-based reason, ADEA's prohibitions of age discrimination are more difficult and less attractive to enforce."[43]

CHAPTER 4

The Trials of Online Job Searching

In today's job market, digital resources and tools have become more important than ever when searching for a job. Using the Internet and social media, job seekers can network with colleagues and potential employers, they can research companies, and they can apply for jobs. According to a 2015 Pew Research Center survey, the Internet has become an essential tool for America's job seekers. Among job seekers who had looked for a job during the two years prior to the July 2015 survey date, 90 percent used the Internet to research jobs and 84 percent applied for a job online. Many of these recent job seekers say that online job resources were the most important tool available to them.

Easier, Quicker, and Cheaper

Most businesses today also rely on online tools for recruitment and hiring. According to a 2017 survey from the Statistics Brain Research Center, an average of 4 million jobs are posted online each month. Those postings lead to a lot of new hires; about 18.6 million people are hired from online job postings each year, the same survey found. Online tools use complex formulas known as algorithms to scan résumés and quickly identify those with the desired skills. For example, if a company is looking for a graphic artist, the online tool would probably tag for further review any résumés that mention Photoshop because this program is an essential graphic arts tool. Those that fail to mention Photoshop would probably go no further. Hundreds of résumés can be narrowed down based on specific job criteria in a few minutes, much faster than reviewing each by hand.

Although these tools make the hiring process easier, quicker, and cheaper, they also allow businesses to screen people by age even before they consider their qualifications. Online job search tools rely on algorithms to help sort through a massive pool of job applicants. In some cases, these software applications screen out more than 70 percent of submitted résumés before a human manager ever sees them. This same technology can also be used to screen out older job applicants. For example, online job applications often have fields for prospective employees to enter birth dates, graduation dates, and/or work experience dates. In many cases, if an applicant leaves these fields blank, they cannot submit the application. These dates serve no purpose other than to give companies information they can use to screen applicants based on age. "Here's the question: Why would you need someone's date of birth? Do you ask them their sex, their race? No," says Cathy Ventrell-Monsees, the senior attorney-adviser to the chair of the EEOC. "If it matters when someone gets a job, perhaps because there are benefits, then you ask for date of birth when they get the job."[44] Age-related questions on online applications may even deter older workers from applying for jobs because they believe they will not be given fair consideration because of their age.

In some cases, employers have adjusted these fields so that they only go back to the 1980s, which has the effect of screening out anyone who graduated or had work experience before that date. In Illinois, Attorney General Lisa Madigan has opened an investigation into several online job search sites after a seventy-year-old called her office to complain that he could not use a résumé-building tool on a job search site because the drop-down menu required him to select the year he graduated or got his first job. The oldest date on the menu was 1980, which excludes job seekers over age fifty-two. In her investigation, Madigan's office has found that although other job search sites were less restrictive, they all had some age limits, which Madigan asserts is discrimination. "Anybody who's alive and wants to look for a job [should] be able to, and be able to put in accurate information,"[45] she says.

To even the playing field, organizations like AARP want the EEOC to make using a required field for date of birth or graduation date illegal. "Any time they're using age in those algorithms that is a violation of the ADEA,"[46] says Laurie McCann of AARP.

In today's job market, digital resources and tools have become more important than ever when searching for a job. A 2015 study estimated that 84 percent of job seekers had applied for a job online.

Digital Natives Wanted

Other times, online job applications can deter older applicants from even applying by stating a preference for digital natives or giving a maximum number of years of experience. The term *digital native* refers to someone who has grown up using technology—like the Internet, computers, and mobile devices. When used in a job posting, it is a not-so-subtle way of saying that older workers need not apply. This is an example of stereotyping older workers as people who do not understand technology and are slow to learn and use it. Yet recent research contradicts this stereotype. In 2016 cloud storage provider Dropbox and market research firm Ipsos Mori surveyed more than four thousand workers in the United States and Europe about their use of technology at work. The survey discovered that workers aged fifty-five and older used an average of 4.9 forms of technology (such as laptops, tablets, and smartphones) each week, slightly higher than the overall average of 4.7 forms.

> "Any time they're using age in those algorithms that is a violation of the ADEA."[46]
>
> —Laurie McCann, an attorney with AARP Foundation Litigation

The survey also found that workers in this same age group were less likely to find using technology at work stressful than younger workers (aged eighteen to thirty-four), who are considered digital natives. When asked about these results, Dropbox's Rob Baesman suggested that older workers may be better able to cope with some of the less-than-perfect technology that is more likely to be found in the workplace. For example, younger workers who are used to effortlessly interacting with Snapchat and Twitter may feel frustrated dealing with an in-house database built twenty years ago. "When you look at the technologies broadly still in use in the workplace, they often don't achieve that level of cleanliness and personability in our personal lives," says Baesman. "So younger people will feel frustration at tools that are not up to snuff."[47]

Recruiting Employees on Social Media

Social media sites are another commonly used tool for job searching and hiring. Businesses use social media to search for job applicants, promote open positions, and screen potential new hires. According to recruiting firm RiseSmart, about 95 percent of employee search firm recruiters use the professional networking site LinkedIn to find job candidates to present to companies looking for top talent. Employers are also using LinkedIn to fill open positions. According to a 2016 survey by the Society for Human Resource Management, 84 percent of company human resources executives use social media to recruit new employees. An additional 9 percent said they planned to start using social media for recruiting in the near future.

In 2017 the world's most-used social media site, Facebook, entered the online job recruitment market. The company added a new job-posting feature for businesses. This feature allows employers to post an unlimited number of job advertisements on their Facebook pages and have users submit applications through the Facebook site. When users apply for a job, Facebook will automatically populate the application with information from their public Facebook profile. Users can then edit the prefilled form and submit it. Hiring companies can easily track and review submitted applications through Facebook, which also generates a Messenger thread between the hiring company and the applicant. "A lot of job seeking behavior is casual, and this doesn't take a huge investment," says Andrew Bosworth, Facebook's vice president of ads and business platform. "These are tools that people want and will make their lives easier."[48]

In addition, companies can also pay a fee to have Facebook promote their job postings in the news feeds of targeted users. One of Facebook's strengths is its ability to target audiences for advertisers and deliver ads to users who are most likely to be interested and respond. The site's new hiring tools offer companies a way to target their job postings, just like

Social Media Is a Top Job Recruitment Tool

Social media has become an essential tool for job recruitment. The percentage of companies using social media for job-recruitment increased from 56 percent in 2011 to 84 percent in 2015, according to a 2016 survey. Although social media is an important job recruitment tool, for most companies, it is one of many methods used to identify and hire new talent.

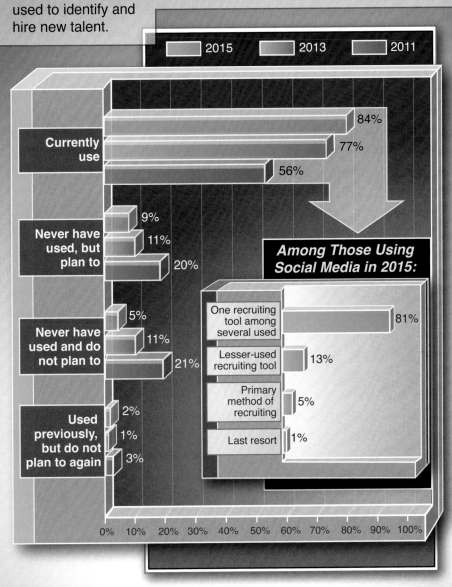

Legend: 2015, 2013, 2011

Currently use
- 84%
- 77%
- 56%

Never have used, but plan to
- 9%
- 11%
- 20%

Never have used and do not plan to
- 5%
- 11%
- 21%

Used previously, but do not plan to again
- 2%
- 1%
- 3%

Among Those Using Social Media in 2015:
- One recruiting tool among several used: 81%
- Lesser-used recruiting tool: 13%
- Primary method of recruiting: 5%
- Last resort: 1%

Note: Percentages may not total 100 percent due to rounding. Respondents who answered "don't know" were excluded from this analysis.

Source: Society for Human Resource Management, "SHRM Survey Findings: Using Social Media for Talent Acquisition—Recruitment and Screening," January 7, 2016. www.shrm.org.

any other advertisement on Facebook, to specific groups of people who meet certain criteria (including personal interests and background). Companies including Verizon, Amazon, and Target (among others) have taken advantage of Facebook's hiring tools to target job ads to a specific audience.

Using Social Media to Discriminate

Although Facebook's targeted job postings were an effective way to get job ads in front of the people who want to see them, they also allowed businesses to discriminate against older workers. This was the finding of a 2017 investigation by the nonprofit news organization ProPublica and the *New York Times*. Their investigation revealed that people over a certain age were prevented from even seeing job postings for which they might have been qualified, simply because of their age. And this was happening with job postings from dozens of US companies—among them Verizon, Amazon, Goldman Sachs, and Target. For example, Verizon placed a job posting on Facebook to recruit applicants for a financial planning and analysis unit. The ad featured a smiling millennial at a computer. The ad was targeted to appear only on the Facebook feeds of people aged twenty-five to thirty-six who lived in or near Washington, DC; had recently visited the capital; and had an interest in finance. Millions of other Facebook users never saw the ad because they did not fit the targeted characteristics, including age.

"Used responsibly, age-based targeting for employment purposes is an accepted industry practice and for good reason: it helps employers recruit and people of all ages find work."[50]

—Rob Goldman, a Facebook vice president

Several legal experts believe that the practice of targeting users by age violates the ADEA, which prohibits discrimination against people aged forty and older in hiring and employment. "It's blatantly unlawful,"[49] says Debra Katz, a Washington, DC, employment lawyer who represents victims of discrimination. Facebook

The Case Against PricewaterhouseCoopers

At age fifty, and with more than ten years of experience as a certified public accountant, Steve Rabin applied for an accounting job at Pricewaterhouse-Coopers (PwC), a global accounting and professional services firm. During an interview at the company, Rabin was asked if he would be able to work for a younger supervisor. Even though he assured the interviewers that he had many good experiences working with and for younger coworkers, Rabin was not hired for the position.

In 2016 Rabin filed an age discrimination lawsuit against the company on behalf of himself and other PwC job applicants aged forty and over. The lawsuit alleges that PwC has engaged in several practices that discriminate against older job applicants, such as primarily hiring entry-level accountants through campus recruiting and web pages that are only accessible to college students. The company did not post these entry-level accounting jobs on its general website and provided no way for someone not affiliated with a college to apply for open positions. In addition, the company's online job application requires applicants to answer questions that make it easy to identify older applicants. The lawsuit alleges that PwC's recruiting and hiring practices have unfairly stacked the deck against older job applicants. Lawyers for PwC say that the firm did not violate the ADEA. In addition, they point out that there are many ways to apply for a job at the accounting firm, not just through campus recruiting.

executives, however, defended their use of targeted ads. "Used responsibly, age-based targeting for employment purposes is an accepted industry practice and for good reason: it helps employers recruit and people of all ages find work,"[50] says Rob Goldman, a Facebook vice president.

Fifty-eight-year-old Mark Edelstein believes that he has been denied opportunities to apply for jobs because the job ads never appeared on his Facebook news feed. Edelstein, a social media marketing strategist who has struggled to find a job since turning fifty, regularly searches online through various sites for potential job leads. While scrolling through his Facebook news feed in December 2017, he saw various ads for goods and services related to his interest in social media marketing. One ad, for instance, promoted the marketing software of a company called HubSpot. He did not think much of it until he learned from the ProPublica/*New York Times* investigation that around the same time he was looking at the HubSpot software ad, the same company had posted a job for a social media director and that posting had been sent to hundreds of Facebook users. It was precisely the type of job he had been looking for, but it was never sent to Edelstein because he did not fit the company's age profile. According to the news media investigation, HubSpot had directed Facebook to target the ad to users between the ages of twenty-seven and forty who lived in the United States. Because Edelstein did not meet the age requirements, he never saw the job posting. "Hypothetically, had I seen a job for a social media director at HubSpot, even if it involved relocation, I ABSOLUTELY would have applied for it,"[51] said Edelstein after he learned about the ad.

When asked about the practice of limiting the ad to a certain age group, a HubSpot spokeswoman responded that the ad was placed on many online sites and was open to any applicant who met the required qualifications, regardless of age or other demographic characteristics. She also said that "the use of the targeted age-range selection on the Facebook ad was frankly a mistake on our part given our lack of experience using that platform for job postings and not a feature we will use again."[52]

The ProPublica/*New York Times* investigation revealed that other tech companies are also allowing employers to discriminate by age. ProPublica was able to purchase job ads on Google and LinkedIn that specifically excluded users older than forty. The tech companies approved the targeted ads without question. When asked about the practice, Google acknowledged that it does not prevent advertisers from targeting recipients based on age.

Google and other digital advertising giants give employers an option to select a specific age range for job ads. Google acknowledges that it does not prevent advertisers from targeting recipients based on age.

Who Is Responsible?

The practice of using age-based targeted job ads online is being challenged in court. In 2017 the Communications Workers of America filed a lawsuit against several US employers, including Amazon, T-Mobile, and Cox Communications. The lawsuit alleged that the companies engaged in age discrimination by putting age limits on people who could see job postings on Facebook, limiting some ads to users younger than thirty-eight years old. "This pattern or practice of discrimination denies job opportunities to individuals who are searching for and interested in jobs, reduces the number of older workers who apply for jobs with the offending employers and employment agencies, and depresses the number of older workers who are hired,"[53] the complaint reads.

Beyond the hiring companies, people believe that social media companies and tech platforms bear some responsibility to monitor how their platforms are being used and ensure that they are not being used to discriminate. In response, Facebook announced in 2017 that it would require advertisers to self-certify that their employment, housing, and credit ads followed antidiscrimination laws. However, the social media company said it would not block companies from purchasing age-targeted ads and did not commit to monitoring the veracity of the self-certifications. LinkedIn also added a self-certification step that prevents employers from using age ranges in job postings unless they certify the ad does not violate discrimination laws.

Legal experts are unsure how much responsibility and potential liability social media companies like Facebook and LinkedIn could have in an age discrimination case. As currently written, the ADEA only holds employers or employment agencies, recruiters, and advertising firms liable. But other antidiscrimination laws, such as the Fair Housing Act, state that publishers can be liable

I, Too, Am Qualified

In Denver, filmmaker and writer Nancy Fingerhood and her husband are using the power of social media to bring attention to age discrimination. Fingerhood says that her own struggle to find a job later in life inspired her and her husband to start the "I, Too, Am Qualified" campaign. "We are both photographers and videographers, and we have experienced what it is like not to get an email reply, let alone an interview, even though our resumes showed our skills matched the desired qualifications," says Fingerhood. The social media campaign encourages older workers to speak up about how age discrimination in the workplace has affected them. It asks the older workers to share their experiences and pictures on the campaign's blog to show how common age discrimination is and to help people realize there are others who understand what they are experiencing.

Nancy Fingerhood and Michael Lindenberger, "Guest Post: I, Too, Am Qualified," *Colorado Independent*, December 14, 2017. www.coloradoindependent.com.

for discriminatory ads. Some legal experts believe that the same liability should extend to social media companies who publish job postings that discriminate by age. In addition, Facebook has been named as one of the defendants in the communication workers' lawsuit. The plaintiff argues that the social media firm operates as an employment agency by collecting and providing data to help employers find suitable candidates, working with employers to create advertising strategies for job postings, and giving employers information about the effectiveness of ads. Regardless of whether the social media company is found responsible under federal law, it could be responsible under state or local statutes. For example, under California's Fair Employment and Housing Act, it is illegal to help, assist, or encourage discriminatory acts as defined by the statute.

Keeping Online Job Searches Fair

The Internet and social media can be effective tools for both job applicants and hiring companies. Online, job seekers can research companies and open positions and quickly submit applications for jobs that they feel are a good fit. Companies can quickly receive and review applications using technology to effectively identify and hire the most qualified candidates. However, hiring companies must take care to ensure that they are not using online tools to enable age discrimination in the workplace.

CHAPTER 5

What Is Being Done About Age Discrimination?

The number of Americans who are sixty-five or older and still working continues to rise. For instance, the percentage of people in that age group working full- or part-time jobs rose from 12.8 percent in 2000 to 18.8 percent in 2016. Not only are more older people working, today's older workers are more likely to be working full-time than peers in previous years, according to a 2016 Pew Research Center analysis of employment data. With more older Americans continuing to make up part of the workforce, fairness in hiring and other employment decisions will continue to be a priority. "With so many more people working and living longer, we can't afford to allow age discrimination to waste the knowledge, skills, and talent of older workers,"[54] says acting EEOC chair Victoria Lipnic.

Calls to Strengthen Laws

Although federal, state, and local laws have tried to address age-based discrimination, discrimination still occurs. Groups such as AARP have called on the EEOC to do a better job of enforcing the ADEA. The group has also urged Congress to pass stronger protections for older workers. In June 2017, the EEOC held a hearing to discuss the ADEA. Attorney Laurie McCann of AARP spoke at the hearing. She expressed her concern that age discrimination is wrongly viewed as somehow less of a problem than other types of bias and that this attitude has resulted in weak laws. "Age discrimination is no less harmful than other forms of discrimination," said McCann. She described the ADEA as a "second-class civil rights law" that provides much less protection for older workers than other civil rights legislation "both in terms of statutory language and how that language has been interpreted by the courts."[55]

> "With so many more people working and living longer, we can't afford to allow age discrimination to waste the knowledge, skills, and talent of older workers."[54]
>
> —Victoria Lipnic, acting EEOC chair

During the hearing, McCann noted that although older workers enjoyed more job opportunities during the fifty years since the ADEA was enacted, many still report seeing or experiencing age discrimination at work. She described several ways in which age discrimination still occurs in the workplace, from blatant hiring discrimination to specifying a maximum number of years of experience, which eliminates older applicants. She also mentioned online job search tools that screen out older applicants, such as by requiring birth dates or graduation dates in online applications. "The newest and perhaps most pernicious frontier of age discrimination in hiring screens, though, may be the use of 'big data'—the collection and compilation of data from multiple sources, to which a robo-recruiting algorithm is applied—to recruit and refer job applicants," said McCann. "Discrimination buried deep in multiple datasets and mathematical algorithms will likely be more difficult to detect. However, at least one study has found that, under such algorithms, age was the biggest predictor of being invited to interview, with the youngest and the oldest applicants least likely to be successful."[56] McCann called on the EEOC to strengthen ADEA protections and enforcement.

Other experts urged the EEOC to get tough on age discrimination because it is causing the country's economic health to suffer. John Challenger, the CEO of the Chicago-based global

The number of Americans who are aged sixty-five and older and still working continues to rise. Additionally, today's older workers are more likely to be working full time than their peers in previous years.

outplacement and career transitioning firm Challenger, Gray & Christmas, testified that keeping older people out of the workforce, especially skilled workers, was damaging the US economy. He suggested that if more skilled older employees kept working, it would significantly reduce the skilled worker shortage in the United States. He urged changes in the law that would make it easier for employees to prove age discrimination. Prior to the Supreme Court's 2009 ruling in *Gross v. FBL Financial*, plaintiffs in an age discrimination lawsuit had to prove that age was only one of several factors that resulted in an adverse employment decision, such as a demotion or decrease in pay. "Today's standard is that age discrimination is the [primary] factor that led to the adverse employment decision, and the plaintiff has the burden of proof. Legislation that restores the previous standard of proof will not only protect older workers, but help reverse some of the negative stereotypes plaguing the workplace,"[57] he said.

Proposing New Legislation

Members of Congress have heeded these suggestions. Over the years, several attempts to propose new legislation to strengthen protections for older workers have been made. In 2017 a bipartisan group of US senators introduced a bill that would make it easier for victims of age discrimination to prove their claims. The Protecting Older Workers Against Discrimination Act was proposed in response to the Supreme Court's *Gross* ruling. In that case, the justices ruled that victims of age discrimination must prove that the discrimination was the sole or primary factor in a negative hiring or employment decision.

Since *Gross*, plaintiffs have had a higher bar to prove age discrimination as compared to other workers who allege discrimination based on race, religion, gender, or national origin. The act would reduce the burden on plaintiffs. It would restore the pre-*Gross* legal standard for age discrimination claims, allowing plaintiffs to prove discrimination as long as age is a factor in an employment decision, even if it is not the sole factor. "All Americans deserve the right to safe conditions and equal rights under the law in their workplaces," says Senator Patrick Leahy of Vermont, one of the bill's cosponsors. As he explains,

> "All Americans deserve the right to safe conditions and equal rights under the law in their workplaces."[58]
>
> —Senator Patrick Leahy of Vermont

The Protecting Older Workers Against Discrimination Act (POWADA) reinforces these fundamental rights for our nation's seniors in particular—rights which were severely restricted in the Supreme Court's *Gross v. FBL Financial* decision. I have long worked to defend the vital protections of the Civil Rights Act, and POWADA is a clearly needed extension of these protections. We must continue to remedy workplace discrimination, and that is all the more necessary when it comes to discrimination against those who are most vulnerable.[58]

Several similar bills have been introduced in Congress since 2009; however, none has been passed and signed into law. The POWADA was referred to the Senate Committee on Health, Education, Labor, and Pensions in 2017 for discussion.

Corporate Programs and Policies

Lawmakers are not the only ones considering actions that can help reduce or eliminate age bias in the workplace. Some companies are adopting their own policies and programs. Some of these focus on recruiting and retaining people of all ages, including older workers. One way to do this is to open up apprenticeship programs to people of all ages, not just younger workers. Huntington Ingalls Industries (HII) is one of the largest military shipbuilding companies in the United States. The firm's apprentice program, the Newport News Shipbuilding Apprentice School, originally had an age limit of twenty-one years old for participants. Over time, the age limit was raised and then eliminated in 1996. Fifty-eight-year-old Charlene DeWindt graduated from the program as an electrician in 2016 and then completed a second apprentice program offered by the company. She now works as a production planner and scheduler for HII. DeWindt says the apprentice program has been life changing. "I had been out of school for 40 years. . . . But I was persistent, and now I have a great job, benefits and a chance to excel," she says. "This program has allowed me the opportunity to learn so much, keep my brain and body active and save more for retirement."[59]

The apprenticeship program also benefits DeWindt's employer. Of the twenty-nine hundred apprentice school alumni currently working for HII's Newport News Shipbuilding division, many are now in leadership positions. HII's efforts to embrace older workers have led to an age-diverse workforce. As of 2016, the HII workforce was made up of 35 percent baby boomers, 32 percent millennials, and 32 percent Generation Xers.

AARP's Employer Pledge Program

AARP has launched a nationwide effort to help employers and workers combat age discrimination. The AARP Employer Pledge Program aims to help pair employers with experienced workers. Companies that take part in the program sign a pledge that says they recognize the importance of equal opportunities for all workers, regardless of age; that workers age fifty and older should be able to equally compete for and be hired for jobs; and the value of experienced workers. They also agree to recruit across diverse age groups and will consider all applicants equally, regardless of their age. More than 460 employers have joined the program, pledging not to discriminate against older workers.

Other companies are focusing on recruiting talent across all age groups to build a diverse and experienced workforce. Several years ago, the UnitedHealth Group, a Minnesota-based managed health care company, recognized that its customer base was aging. Executives realized that a workforce that reflected the age of its customers might lead to improved communication, which would benefit the company. The UnitedHealth Group created a talent recruitment strategy that actively works to attract employees of all ages. The company recruits younger workers on college campuses and through student internship programs. It also targets older workers through recruiting that targets veterans and military spouses. The company also specifically seeks to recruit workers aged fifty and older.

Some companies have implemented programs that make it easier for older people to reenter the workforce after an extended absence. Centrica PLC is an energy company based in the United Kingdom. With thirty-seven thousand employees worldwide, the company places a priority on attracting and retaining talent of all ages. One of its innovative recruiting programs is the HitReturn program. HitReturn targets senior-level professionals who want to return to work after a break of two years or more.

Aging-Friendly Workplaces

More than half of workers in all age groups describe their employers as "aging-friendly," according to a 2017 survey. An aging-friendly workplace is one that offers employees new and interesting assignments, possibility of promotion, flexible work arrangements, and training—regardless of age. In contrast, 21 percent of workers (from all age groups) deemed their employers not to be aging-friendly. Survey results were remarkably consistent when broken down by age group.

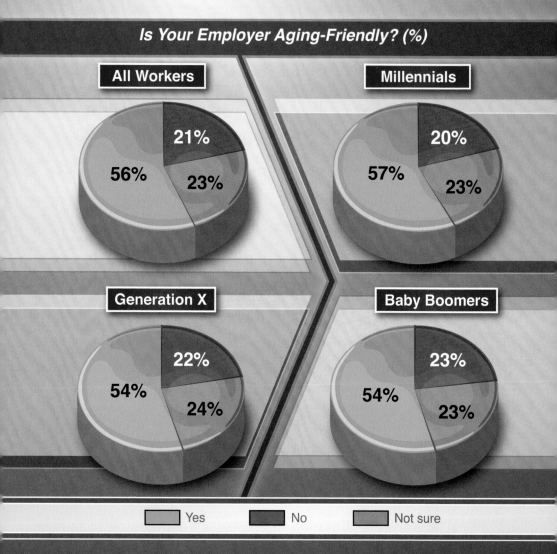

Is Your Employer Aging-Friendly? (%)

All Workers
- 21%
- 23%
- 56%

Millennials
- 20%
- 23%
- 57%

Generation X
- 22%
- 24%
- 54%

Baby Boomers
- 23%
- 23%
- 54%

Yes   No   Not sure

Note: Baby boomers are usually identified as people who were born between 1946 and 1964. Generation X is usually identified as individuals who were born between 1965 and 1980. Millennials are usually identified as people who were born between 1981 and 1996.

Source: Transamerica Center for Retirement Studies, "Wishful Thinking or Within Reach? Three Generations Prepare for 'Retirement,'" December 2017. www.transamericacenter.org.

The program offers so-called returnships—paid twelve-week internships—which give older workers the chance to work on a professional assignment and meet with a mentor. Although there is no guarantee, HitReturn can lead to a permanent job.

Working Together Across Generations

Helping older and younger employees work together effectively can reduce stereotypes and discrimination in the workplace. At the UnitedHealth Group, all employees are required to complete an online training course that focuses on diversity and inclusion. One section of the course highlights the differences in work styles and approaches for people from different generations. By increasing employee awareness about the different work styles, the training aims to help employees more effectively communicate and work together, regardless of age. The company also hosts several diversity and inclusion webinars each year for its workforce.

Companies like PNC Financial Services Group have created cross-generation mentorship programs to foster communication and teamwork among employees of all ages. At PNC, the Diversity and Inclusion Mentoring Program matches older workers with younger workers for a period of one year. Once matched, the mentor and mentee agree upon the frequency and format of their mentoring meetings and what they will work on together. Sue Filiczkowski, a forty-eight-year-old senior underwriting manager, says that the program has been very rewarding. Over the past year, she has helped her mentee, a millennial, overcome a fear of doing presentations for large groups of people. Eventually, Filiczkowski's mentee felt confident enough to lead a presentation for the company's senior managers. During the pair's regular meetings, they also bonded by reading articles about leadership and work challenges. "We would discuss what we got out of the articles and how we would have responded to similar situations at PNC,"[60] says Filiczkowski. Together, they worked to solve problems they both faced at work.

PNC also has an Employee Business Resource Group known as IGen, which focuses on intergenerational issues. Through this group, workers of various ages can share and transfer knowledge. In addition, IGen is working with the company's talent development team to share personal stories and best practices about career experiences. They hope this partnership will help PNC hire and retain the most talented workers, regardless of age.

Becoming a Valuable Asset

Knowing that age bias is always out there, many older workers are taking matters into their own hands; they are taking steps to make themselves valuable assets at work. One important step for employees of all ages is to keep up-to-date on the latest industry and technology trends. Employees can keep their skills sharp by attending industry conferences, taking technology training courses, and reading the latest industry news. According to a 2016 survey of more than twenty-two hundred CEOs across the United States, the desire to learn new skills is the most important factor for success in today's workplace. "Successful people never stop learning," says Bill Driscoll, a district president for Accountemps, a temporary staffing firm that commissioned the survey. "The world is changing quickly and constantly, and it's vital to stay informed of the latest trends and sought-after skills in your industry. If you can do multiple things and learn multiple things, then you can have a lot of different options, career-wise, and be that much more valuable to the company."[61] Staying current on the latest technology is a good way to fight stereotypes of older workers being out of touch; it can also make them stand out from other employees and become more valuable to bosses.

"Successful people never stop learning. The world is changing quickly and constantly, and it's vital to stay informed of the latest trends and sought-after skills in your industry."[61]

—Bill Driscoll, a district president for Accountemps, a temporary staffing firm

According to a 2017 survey from the Transamerica Center for Retirement Studies, baby boomer employees say that they are taking a variety of steps to ensure they can continue working long past age sixty-five. More than half of all boomers report that they are taking care of their health (68 percent) and are performing well at their current job (59 percent). Slightly less than half said they are taking steps to keep their job skills current and up-to-date (42 percent). At the same time, only 14 percent are keeping up with their professional network, and a scant 4 percent are going back to school to learn new skills.

Keeping in touch with a professional and personal network is also important. Todd Williams ran his own business when he adopted his two young granddaughters. With two children to support, fifty-nine-year-old Williams decided to look for a more stable work situation, one that provided a steady salary, life and health

A recent survey revealed that baby boomer employees are taking a variety of steps to ensure that they can continue to work far beyond age sixty-five. In addition to keeping their job skills relevant, some are even going back to school to learn new skills.

insurance, and some paid time off. Immediately, he turned to the professional network that he had built up over his years as a business owner. Williams says networking "has landed more contracts that meet my needs. It also has me in the running for two . . . jobs that have not been posted—and may never be posted—as they are creating positions for me."[62] Williams believes that older workers may have an advantage because they have had years to grow a much bigger network than younger workers.

Becoming an Entrepreneur

Some workers, fed up with age discrimination and other barriers in the workplace, decide to use their skills to start their own businesses or take on consulting or freelance work. "I retired from a very lucrative career because my age was holding me back from finding a new job," says first-time entrepreneur and baby boomer Dick Kuiper. "I tried unsuccessfully to find a new position that

Reverse Mentorship

In some companies, reverse mentorships are helping to bridge the gap between different generations at work. In companies such as Cisco Systems, Target, and UnitedHealth Group, millennials often play the role of technology consultant to other employees who may be less comfortable with technology. In one example, Phyllis Korkki, an assignment editor at the *New York Times* who is in her midfifties, reached out to a twenty-seven-year-old coworker to help her learn the ins and outs of the Snapchat app, which was being used as a newsroom tool to reach new readers. The reverse mentorship with the younger coworker helped her learn the basics of a new technology and incorporate it into her work. "It also made me realize that organizations and individual workers could do a lot more to bridge the gaps between generations. Each age group has untapped resources that can benefit others at a different stage of life," says Korkki.

Phyllis Korkki, "What Could I Possibly Learn from a Mentor Half My Age? Plenty," *New York Times*, September 10, 2016. www.nytimes.com.

would pay me a living wage in a traditional job in that career field. Then I thought, 'Why not create my own job?' I did. It worked and I'm off and running with a successful business of my own that's partially linked to my previous career."[63]

Older entrepreneurs often have experience, financial stability, and a large network of professional contacts—all of which are extremely valuable when starting a business. In fact, nearly one-fourth of new entrepreneurs in 2016 were between the ages of fifty-five and sixty-four, according to the Kaufmann Index of Entrepreneurship. "The middle-aged entrepreneur has a formidable range of weaponry to use against his young competitors, including depth of experience, wisdom, accumulated wealth and confidence,"[64] says Roger St. Pierre, a senior vice president at First Western Federal Savings Bank.

> "The middle-aged entrepreneur has a formidable range of weaponry to use against his young competitors, including depth of experience, wisdom, accumulated wealth and confidence."[64]
>
> —Roger St. Pierre, a senior vice president at First Western Federal Savings Bank

A Valuable Resource

Older workers can greatly benefit companies with their wealth of skills and experience and vast professional networks. As people are living longer and healthier lives, these workers have many more productive years ahead of them. By recognizing these workers as assets instead of liabilities, companies can help break down the barriers of age discrimination and benefit from this often underutilized and valuable resource.

SOURCE NOTES

Introduction: Too Old to Work?

1. Quoted in Patrick G. Lee and Carol Hymowitz, "Texas Roadhouse Age Discrimination Lawsuit Could Affect Hiring Practices," *Bloomberg Businessweek*, September 24, 2015. www.bloomberg.com.
2. Quoted in Peter Gosselin, "Federal Court May Decide If Employers Can Reject Older Job Seekers to Protect 'Image,'" ProPublica, January 31, 2017. www.propublica.org.
3. Quoted in Lee and Hymowitz, "Texas Roadhouse Age Discrimination Lawsuit Could Affect Hiring Practices."
4. Quoted in Lee and Hymowitz, "Texas Roadhouse Age Discrimination Lawsuit Could Affect Hiring Practices."
5. Quoted in US Equal Employment Opportunity Commission, "Texas Roadhouse to Pay $12 Million to Settle EEOC Age Discrimination Lawsuit," March 31, 2017. www.eeoc.gov.
6. Quoted in Patricia Reaney, "Ageism in US Workplace: A Persistent Problem Unlikely to Go Away," Reuters, October 19, 2015. www.reuters.com.
7. Quoted in Bob Sullivan, "For Older Workers, Getting a New Job Is a Crapshoot," CNBC.com, July 7, 2016. www.cnbc.com.
8. Quoted in Teresa Wiltz, "Age Discrimination Hard to Prove," *Detroit News*, September 27, 2015. www.detroitnews.com.
9. Quoted in US Equal Employment Opportunity Commission, "Texas Roadhouse to Pay $12 Million to Settle EEOC Age Discrimination Lawsuit."

Chapter 1: How Serious a Problem Is Age Discrimination?

10. Quoted in Reaney, "Ageism in US Workplace."

11. Quoted in Liz Ryan, "The Ugly Truth About Age Discrimination," *Forbes*, January 31, 2014. www.forbes.com.

12. Quoted in Gary Rotstein, "Workforce Keeps Aging, but It Doesn't Mean Age Discrimination Cases Disappear," *Pittsburgh Post-Gazette*, October 31, 2016. www.post-gazette.com.

13. Quoted in Peter Gosselin and Ariana Tobin, "Inside IBM's Purge of Thousands of Workers Who Have One Thing in Common," *Mother Jones*, March 22, 2018. www.motherjones.com.

14. Quoted in Justin Criado, "Hospital Settles Age-Discrimination Suit," *Telluride (CO) Daily Planet*, January 10, 2018. www.telluridenews.com.

15. Quoted in Criado, "Hospital Settles Age-Discrimination Suit."

16. Quoted in Jon Swartz, "Ageism Is Forcing Many to Look Outside Silicon Valley, but Tech Hubs Offer Little Respite," *USA Today*, August 4, 2017. www.usatoday.com.

17. Quoted in Swartz, "Ageism Is Forcing Many to Look Outside Silicon Valley, but Tech Hubs Offer Little Respite."

18. Quoted in John McDermott, "Age Discrimination in the Workplace Is on the Rise—but It's Hard to Prove," *Mel Magazine*, December 6, 2016. https://melmagazine.com.

19. Quoted in Shareen Pathak, "'I Was Invisible': How Agency Ageism Affects Those 50-plus," Digiday.com, August 11, 2016. https://digiday.com.

20. Quoted in Pathak, "'I Was Invisible.'"

21. Quoted in Pathak, "'I Was Invisible.'"

22. Quoted in CBS News, "Age Discrimination Is Alive and Well," March 3, 2017. www.cbsnews.com.

23. Quoted in Ina Jaffe, "Too Much Experience to Be Hired? Some Older Americans Face Age Bias," NPR, March 24, 2017. www.npr.org.

24. Quoted in David Neumark, "Do Women Face Age Discrimination in the Job Market? Absolutely. Here's Proof," *Los Angeles Times*, April 26, 2016. www.latimes.com.

25. Quoted in Cindy Krischer Goodman, "More People Are Working Past Retirement Age. That Means Big Challenges for Businesses," *Miami Herald*, October 2, 2016. www.miamiherald.com.

Chapter 2: How Are People Hurt by Age Discrimination?

26. Quoted in Andrew Flowers, "Age Discrimination in the Job Market May Hurt Women More," FiveThirtyEight.com, November 30, 2015. https://fivethirtyeight.com.

27. Quoted in Kerry Hannon, "Older Job Seekers Find Ways to Avoid Age Bias," *New York Times*, January 16, 2015. www.nytimes.com.

28. Quoted in Jackie Keast, "The Age Paradox: Older People Want to Work, but Age Discrimination Stands in Their Way," Australian Ageing Agenda, August 5, 2015. www.australianageingagenda.com.au.

29. Quoted in Keast, "The Age Paradox."

30. David Neumark, Ian Burn, and Patrick Button, "Is It Harder for Older Workers to Find Jobs? New and Improved Evidence from a Field Experiment," National Bureau of Economic Research, October 2015. www.nber.org.

31. Quoted in Ronnie Cohen, "Older Women Get the Brush-Off from Potential Employers," Reuters, March 15, 2017. www.reuters.com.

Chapter 3: How Does the Law Address Age Discrimination?

32. Quoted in Elizabeth Olsen, "Shown the Door, Older Workers Find Bias Hard to Prove," *New York Times*, August 7, 2017. www.nytimes.com.

33. Quoted in Olsen, "Shown the Door, Older Workers Find Bias Hard to Prove."

34. Quoted in Jeremy J. Glenn and Katelan E. Little, "A Study of the Age Discrimination in Employment Act of 1967," *GP Solo*, November/December 2014, vol. 31, no. 6. www.americanbar.org.

35. US Equal Employment Opportunity Commission, "The Age Discrimination in Employment Act of 1967." www.eeoc.gov.

36. Quoted in US Equal Employment Opportunity Commission, "Court Orders Hawaii HealthCare Professionals and Its Owner to Pay over $190,000 for Age Discrimination," July 19, 2012. www.eeoc.gov.

37. Quoted in US Equal Employment Opportunity Commission, "Court Orders Hawaii HealthCare Professionals and Its Owner to Pay over $190,000 for Age Discrimination."

38. Quoted in US Equal Employment Opportunity Commission, "Court Orders Hawaii HealthCare Professionals and Its Owner to Pay over $190,000 for Age Discrimination."

39. Quoted in US Equal Employment Opportunity Commission, "Advance Components Settles EEOC Age Discrimination Lawsuit," May 18, 2012. www.eeoc.gov.

40. Quoted in US Equal Employment Opportunity Commission, "Advance Components Settles EEOC Age Discrimination Lawsuit."

41. Quoted in Wiltz, "Age Discrimination Hard to Prove."

42. Quoted in Wiltz, "Age Discrimination Hard to Prove."

43. Quoted in Rex Huppke, "Is Your Workplace Ageist?" *Chicago Tribune*, March 25, 2013. http://articles.chicagotribune.com.

Chapter 4: The Trials of Online Job Searching

44. Quoted in Lauren Rosenblatt, "If You Weren't Raised in the Internet Age, You May Need to Worry About Workplace Age Discrimination," *Los Angeles Times*, June 26, 2017. www.latimes.com.

45. Quoted in Ina Jaffe, "Older Workers Find Age Discrimination Built Right into Some Job Websites," NPR, March 28, 2017. www.npr.org.

46. Quoted in Rosenblatt, "If You Weren't Raised in the Internet Age, You May Need to Worry About Workplace Age Discrimination."

47. Quoted in David Z. Morris, "Survey: Older Workers Are Actually More Comfortable with Technology," *Fortune*, August 7, 2016. http://fortune.com.

48. Quoted in Kathleen Chaykowski, "Facebook Unveils Job Postings and Applications, Taking on LinkedIn, Glassdoor," *Forbes*, February 15, 2017. www.forbes.com.

49. Quoted in Julia Angwin, Noam Scheiber, and Ariana Tobin, "Dozens of Companies Are Using Facebook to Exclude Older Workers from Job Ads," ProPublica, December 20, 2017. www.propublica.org.

50. Quoted in Angwin, Scheiber, and Tobin, "Dozens of Companies Are Using Facebook to Exclude Older Workers from Job Ads."

51. Quoted in Angwin, Scheiber, and Tobin, "Dozens of Companies Are Using Facebook to Exclude Older Workers from Job Ads."

52. Quoted in Angwin, Scheiber, and Tobin, "Dozens of Companies Are Using Facebook to Exclude Older Workers from Job Ads."

53. Quoted in Mallory Shelbourne, "Union Sues over Facebook Job Ads That Exclude Older People," *Hill*, December 21, 2017. http://thehill.com.

Chapter 5: What Is Being Done About Age Discrimination?

54. Quoted in Pamela Wolf, "Age Discrimination Is a Barrier to Both Hiring and Further Economic Growth," Employment Law Daily. www.employmentlawdaily.com.

55. Quoted in David Frank, "Feds Must Do More to Fight Age Discrimination," AARP, June 16, 2017. www.aarp.org.

56. US Equal Employment Opportunity Commission, "Written Testimony of Laurie McCann, Senior Attorney, AARP Foundation Litigation," June 14, 2017. www.eeoc.gov.

57. US Equal Employment Opportunity Commission, "Written Testimony of John Challenger, CEO, Challenger, Gray & Christmas, Inc.," June 14, 2017. www.eeoc.gov.

58. Quoted in Chuck Grassley, "Bipartisan Group of Senators Introduce Legislation to Protect Older Workers from Discrimination," February 27, 2017. www.grassley.senate.gov.

59. Quoted in Kerry Hannon, "5 Workplaces That Embrace Older Workers," *Forbes*, November 18, 2016. www.forbes.com.

60. Quoted in Hannon, "5 Workplaces That Embrace Older Workers."

61. Quoted in Kathy Gurchiek, "HR Can Prevent Older Workers from Becoming 'Tech Dinosaurs,'" Society for Human Resource Management, September 29, 2016. www.shrm.org.

62. Quoted in Anne Loehr, "Five Ways Older Workers Can Combat Age Discrimination," *Fast Company*, December 11, 2016. www.fastcompany.com.

63. Quoted in Loehr, "Five Ways Older Workers Can Combat Age Discrimination."

64. Roger St. Pierre, "How Older Entrepreneurs Can Turn Age to Their Advantage," *Entrepreneur*, May 26, 2017. www.entrepreneur.com.

ORGANIZATIONS AND WEBSITES

American Association of Retired Persons (AARP)

601 E St. NW
Washington, DC 20049
website: www.aarp.org

AARP is a nonprofit social welfare organization that advocates for the elderly and how they can continue to enjoy full lives. Its website offers a variety of information, articles, and fact sheets about age discrimination and the workplace.

Civil Rights Center

US Department of Labor
200 Constitution Ave. NW, Room N-4123
Washington, DC 20210
website: www.dol.gov/oasam/programs/crc/index.htm

A division of the US Department of Labor, the Civil Rights Center is responsible for administering and enforcing various civil rights laws, including age discrimination laws.

National Council on Aging

251 Eighteenth St. S., Suite 500
Arlington, VA 22202
website: www.scoa.org

The National Council on Aging is a nonprofit organization that partners with other nonprofit organizations, government, and businesses to provide innovative community programs and services, online help, and advocacy for older Americans.

Senior Service America

8403 Colesville Rd., Suite 200
Silver Spring, MD 20910
website: www.seniorserviceamerica.org

Senior Service America is one of America's oldest and largest operators of employment programs for America's seniors. Its website provides information and news about employment, legislation, and other topics of interest to older workers.

Society for Human Resource Management (SHRM)

website: www.shrm.org

The SHRM is the world's largest human resource professional society, representing 285,000 members in more than 165 countries. Its website offers resources and articles regarding workplace issues, including age discrimination.

US Equal Employment Opportunity Commission (EEOC)

131 M St. NE
Washington, DC 20507
website: www.eeoc.gov

The EEOC enforces federal laws that make it illegal to discriminate against a job applicant or an employee because of the person's race, color, religion, sex, national origin, age (forty or older), disability, or genetic information. Its website includes information about age discrimination and lawsuits filed with the EEOC.

FOR FURTHER RESEARCH

Books

Joseph F. Coughlin, *The Longevity Economy: Unlocking the World's Fastest-Growing, Most Misunderstood Market*. New York: PublicAffairs, 2017.

Margaret Morganroth Gullette, *Ending Ageism, or How Not to Shoot Old People*. New Brunswick, NJ: Rutgers University Press, 2017.

Kerry Hannon, *Great Jobs for Everyone 50+: Finding Work That Keeps You Happy and Healthy . . . and Pays the Bills*. Hoboken, NJ: Wiley, 2012.

Daniel Lyons, *Disrupted: My Misadventure in the Start-Up Bubble*. New York: Hachette, 2016.

Lawrence R. Samuel, *Aging in America: A Cultural History*. Philadelphia: University of Pennsylvania Press, 2017.

Internet Sources

Transamerica Center for Retirement Studies, "Wishful Thinking or Within Reach? Three Generations Prepare for 'Retirement,'" December 2017. www.transamericacenter.org/docs /default-source/retirement-survey-of-workers/tcrs2017_sr _three-generations_prepare_for_retirement.pdf.

Lori A. Trawinski, "Disrupting Aging in the Workplace," AARP Public Policy Institute. www.aarp.org/ppi/info-2016 /disrupting-aging-in-the-workplace.html.

US Equal Employment Opportunity Commission, "Facts About Age Discrimination." www.eeoc.gov/eeoc/publications /age.cfm.

US Equal Employment Opportunity Commission, "Meeting of June 14, 2017—the ADEA @ 50—More Relevant than Ever." www.eeoc.gov/eeoc/meetings/6-14-17/index.cfm.

US Senate Special Committee on Aging, "America's Aging Workforce: Opportunities and Challenges," December 6, 2017. www.aging.senate.gov/hearings/americas-aging-workforce -opportunities-and-challenges.

INDEX

Note: Boldface page numbers indicate illustrations.

PICTURE CREDITS